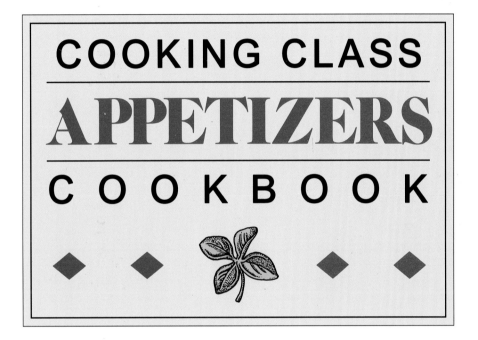

COOKING CLASS

APPETIZERS

COOKBOOK

PUBLICATIONS INTERNATIONAL, LTD.

Pyrex is a registered trademark of Corning Incorporated, Corning, NY 14831.

Photography on pages 19, 23, 27, 33, 39 and 43 by Vuksanovich, Chicago.

Remaining photography by Sacco Productions Limited, Chicago.

Pictured on the front cover (*clockwise from top right*): Hot 'n' Honeyed Chicken Wings (*page 84*), Scallops à la Schaller (*page 72*), Spinach-Cheese Triangles (*page 42*) and Chilled Seafood Lasagna with Herbed Cheese (*page 36*).

Pictured on the inside front cover: Southwest Appetizer Cheesecake (*page 26*).

Pictured on the back cover: Chinese Vegetable Rolls (*page 48*).

Manufactured in the U.S.A.

8 7 6 5 4 3 2 1

ISBN: 0-7853-0190-9

The publishers would like to thank the following companies and organizations for the use of their recipes in this publication: American Egg Board; American Lamb Council; Arkansas Rice Festival; Black-Eyed Pea Jamboree--Athens, Texas; California Tomato Board; Castroville Artichoke Festival; Florida Tomato Committee; The Fresh Garlic Association; Kraft General Foods, Inc.; Thomas J. Lipton Co.; National Sunflower Association; New Jersey Department of Agriculture; North Dakota Beef Commission; North Dakota Wheat Commission; Pace Foods, Inc.; Pennsylvania Fresh Mushroom Program; Pollio Dairy Products; The Quaker Oats Company; St. Mary's County National Oyster Cook-off; Sargento Cheese Company, Inc.; Wisconsin Milk Marketing Board.

CONTENTS

Golden Tomato Soup (*page 16*)

Jumbo Shells Seafood Fancies (*page 32*)

Turkey-Cheese Surprises (*page 82*)

CLASS NOTES

Appetizers, hors d'oeuvres, finger foods—whichever term you use, these tasty tidbits do much more than just tide guests over until dinner. In fact, the word *hors d'oeuvres* means "outside the main meal"—they set the stage for the meal that is to follow. These delicious appetite enhancers are versatile enough to provide party sustenance on their own at an open house, satisfy cravings for midnight munchies or just awaken the appetite in a refreshing first course. However you decide to serve them, appetizers are meant to be enjoyed by both the guests and the cook. The preparation of these menu additions need not be overwhelming. Some simple, up-front planning combined with the step-by-step recipes in *Cooking Class Appetizers* will help to maintain the cook's composure and create a relaxed, festive atmosphere.

When serving appetizers before a meal, keep in mind they are meant to tease the appetite, not satisfy it. One or two selections should be ample, allowing five to seven servings per person. Prepare recipes that contrast in texture, temperature and flavor with the meal that follows. For example, a cold seafood hors d'oeuvre would be a refreshing opener before a main course highlighting roast beef or steak. However, if you are planning an ethnic dinner, coordinating an appetizer from the same foreign country provides a memorable beginning. Many people prefer to serve first-course appetizers before the guests are seated at the dinner table, as this allows the cook time to make last-minute meal preparations. However, starters such as soups and marinated salads should always be served when guests are seated.

For a cocktail party or open house where appetizers are served as the main event, plan a variety of snacks and spreads, including some that are hearty and filling. Remember, too, that the longer the occasion lasts, the more your guests will eat. Plan on ten to twelve servings per person as a minimum. Cold appetizers, such as dips and marinated vegetables, should be made at least several hours to one day ahead since their flavor actually improves with time. Some hot appetizers can be cooked ahead and simply reheated just before serving, while others must be prepared at the last moment. Be sure to enlist kitchen help, if necessary, to give these final details the attention they require. If the food on your appetizer table will be sitting out for several hours, it is important, for food safety reasons, to maintain serving temperatures. Appetizers that need to remain chilled, such as shrimp cocktail, should be served on a platter set over cracked ice. Transfer hot appetizers, such as meatballs, from the oven or rangetop to a warming device, such as a chafing dish or fondue pot for serving. Prepare a balance of hot and cold appetizers that provide a range of flavors and textures, from spicy and rich to light and refreshing. And keep in mind that at a large party where seating is limited, guests appreciate finger food and bite-size portions with not-too-drippy sauces.

Part of the fun in serving hors d'oeuvres is in the presentation. The beautiful photographs in *Cooking Class Appetizers* will give you some eye-catching ideas for finishing touches. A simple spray of small flowers or a handful of fresh herbs provides a colorful garnish on everything from a rustic woven basket to a formal silver platter. A cheese tray or spread surrounded by an array of crisp crackers and thin-sliced breads is also attractive. Another option for garnishing is to choose one of the recipe's ingredients, for example, red onions or cucumbers, and save a few pretty slices as a special finishing touch for the top of the dish.

Following are a few suggestions for first-course appetizers and some easy and delicious entertaining ideas. The football party and open house menus can easily be supplemented with a deli tray or thinly sliced ham, depending on the number of guests and the length of the party. You may wish to serve a variety of flavored coffees and an assortment of delightful cookies as the gathering draws to a close.

First-Course Starters
(Serve any one of the following recipes)
Sherried Oyster and Brie Soup (page 24)
Scampi alla "Fireman Chef" (page 38)
Plentiful "P's" Salad (page 30)
Chinese Vegetable Rolls (page 48)
Chilled Seafood Lasagna with
    Herbed Cheese (page 36)

Midnight Movie Munchies
Cheesy Sun Crisps (page 68)
Harvest-Time Popcorn (page 70)
Liptauer Cheese Appetizer (page 92)
Chicken 'n' Rice Pizza (page 60)

Fall Football Party
Taco Dip (page 54)
Hot 'n' Honeyed Chicken Wings (page 84)
Chilled Seafood Antipasto (page 74)
Cheesy Onion Focaccia (page 45)

Holiday Open House
Southwest Appetizer Cheesecake (page 26)
Microwave Oriental Relish Dip (page 56)
Shrimp Mold (page 90)
Spinach-Cheese Triangles (page 42)
Sesame-Sour Cream Meatballs (page 79)
Egg Champignons (page 40)

Picante Onion Soup

2 large onions
1 clove garlic
¼ cup butter or margarine
2 cups tomato juice
1 can (10½ ounces) condensed beef broth*
1 soup can water
½ cup Pace® picante sauce
1 cup unseasoned croutons (optional)
1 cup (4 ounces) shredded Monterey Jack cheese (optional)
Additional Pace® picante sauce for serving

*May substitute 2⅔ cups ready-to-serve beef broth for the condensed beef broth and water.

1. To slice onions, peel skin and cut each onion in half through the root. Place, cut side down, on cutting board. Cut thin, vertical slices the length of each onion. Cut enough onion slices to measure 3 cups. Set aside.

2. Trim off end of garlic clove. To loosen garlic peel, crush clove with flat side of a large knife. Remove peel and discard.** Mince garlic into small pieces.

3. Place onions, garlic and butter in 3-quart saucepan. Cook and stir over medium-low heat 20 minutes or until onions are tender and golden brown.

4. Stir in tomato juice, broth, water and ½ cup picante sauce. Bring to a boil over medium-high heat. Reduce heat to low. Simmer, uncovered, 20 minutes.

5. Ladle soup into bowls and sprinkle with croutons and cheese. Serve with additional picante sauce. *Makes 6 servings*

**To peel garlic clove in microwave, place clove in small custard cup. Microwave at HIGH (100% power) until slightly softened, 5 to 10 seconds. Slip the clove out of its skin.

Step 1. Slicing onions.

Step 2. Crushing garlic clove to remove peel.

Step 3. Cooking and stirring onion mixture until onions are golden brown.

Potato-Cheese Soup

1 small onion
2 cups water
2 cups red potatoes, peeled and
  cut into cubes
3 tablespoons butter or
  margarine
3 tablespoons all-purpose flour
  Creole seasoning to taste
  Ground red pepper to taste
  Black pepper to taste
3 cups milk
1 cup (4 ounces) shredded
  Cheddar cheese
1½ cups cubed cooked ham
  Chopped fresh parsley for
  garnish

1. To chop onion in food processor, peel and quarter onion; place in bowl. Pulse 4 to 7 times until onion is finely chopped. Scrape bowl once during chopping. Drain onions, if needed. Set aside. (See page 14 for chopping technique with knife.)

2. Bring water to a boil in large saucepan over medium-high heat. Add potatoes and cook until tender when pierced with fork, 13 to 15 minutes.

3. Meanwhile, melt butter in large skillet over medium heat. Add onion; cook and stir 4 to 5 minutes until onion is tender but not brown. Add flour. Season with Creole seasoning, red pepper and black pepper; cook and stir 3 to 4 minutes. Set aside.

4. Drain potatoes, reserving 1 cup liquid. (Add water to make 1 cup, if necessary.)

5. Gradually add potatoes, reserved liquid and milk to onion mixture; stir well.

6. Add cheese and ham. Bring to a boil over medium heat. Reduce heat to low. Simmer 30 minutes, stirring frequently. Garnish, if desired.   *Makes 12 servings*

Step 1. Chopping onion in food processor.

Step 2. Testing tenderness of potatoes.

Step 4. Draining potatoes and reserving 1 cup liquid.

Black-Eyed Pea Soup

2 pounds dried East Texas
    Black-Eyed Peas
2 large potatoes
4 medium onions, thinly sliced
    (page 8)
4 carrots, thinly sliced
½ pound bacon, diced (page 14)
8 quarts water
2 cups thinly sliced celery
2 whole jalapeño peppers
4 bay leaves
½ teaspoon dried thyme leaves,
    crushed
1 meaty ham bone
    Salt and black pepper to taste

1. Rinse black-eyed peas under cold running water. Drain and set aside.

2. To grate potatoes, remove potato skins with paring knife or vegetable peeler. Grate potatoes using medium holes on a box-shaped grater. Place grated potatoes in large bowl of ice water. Set aside.

3. Combine onions, carrots and bacon in large stockpot. Cook and stir over medium-high heat until onions are golden.

4. Drain potatoes. Add black-eyed peas, water, potatoes, celery, jalapeño peppers, bay leaves, thyme and ham bone to onion mixture. Season with salt and black pepper. Bring to a boil. Reduce heat to low. Simmer, covered, 3 to 4 hours. Remove and discard jalapeño peppers and bay leaves.

5. Remove ham bone from soup. Let stand at room temperature until cool enough to handle. Cut meat from ham bone and chop into bite-size pieces. Return meat to stockpot.

6. Adjust seasonings; reheat if necessary.

Makes 12 to 16 servings

Step 2. Grating potatoes.

Step 3. Cooking and stirring onion mixture until onions are golden.

Step 5. Cutting meat from ham bone and chopping into bite-size pieces.

Picante Black Bean Soup

4 slices bacon
1 large onion
1 clove garlic, minced (page 8)
2 cans (15 ounces each) black
   beans, undrained
1 can (about 14 ounces) beef
   broth
1¼ cups water
¾ cup Pace® picante sauce
½ to 1 teaspoon salt
½ teaspoon dried oregano leaves,
   crushed
   Sour cream
   Crackers and additional Pace®
   picante sauce for serving

1. Using scissors, cut through several slices of bacon at once, cutting into ½ × ½-inch pieces. Set aside.

2. Peel skin from onion; cut in half through the root. Place, cut side down, on cutting board. To coarsely chop onion, hold knife horizontally. Make cuts parallel to board, almost to root end. Make vertical, lengthwise cuts of desired thickness. Slice across cuts to root end. (The closer the cuts are spaced, the finer the onion is chopped.) Set aside. (See page 10 for chopping technique with food processor.)

3. Cook and stir bacon in Dutch oven over medium-high heat until crisp. Remove with slotted spoon; drain on paper towels. Set bacon aside.

4. Add onion and garlic to drippings in Dutch oven; cook and stir 3 minutes.

5. Add beans with liquid, broth, water, ¾ cup picante sauce, salt and oregano. Bring to a boil. Reduce heat to low. Simmer, covered, 20 minutes.

6. Ladle into soup bowls; dollop with sour cream. Sprinkle with bacon. Serve with crackers and additional picante sauce.

Makes 6 to 8 servings

Step 1. Cutting several slices of bacon into ½ × ½-inch pieces.

Step 2. Chopping onion with knife.

Step 3. Removing bacon from Dutch oven with slotted spoon.

Golden Tomato Soup

8 medium tomatoes
4 teaspoons reduced-calorie
  margarine
1 cup chopped onion (page 14)
2 cloves garlic, coarsely chopped
  (page 8)
½ cup chopped carrots
¼ cup chopped celery
6 cups chicken broth
¼ cup uncooked rice
2 tablespoons tomato paste
1 tablespoon Worcestershire
  sauce
½ teaspoon dried thyme leaves,
  crushed
¼ to ½ teaspoon black pepper
5 drops hot pepper sauce
  Fresh thyme sprigs for garnish

1. To easily remove tomato peels, cut a skin-deep "x" in each blossom end and place, 1 at a time, in saucepan of simmering water for 10 seconds. (Add about 30 seconds if tomato is not fully ripened.) Remove with slotted spoon; plunge immediately into bowl of cold water for another 10 seconds. (Do not add more than 1 tomato at a time to hot water, or temperature will drop rapidly and cause tomatoes to stew before their skins can be removed.)

2. Remove tomato peels with paring knife. To seed tomatoes, cut each tomato in half horizontally. Hold each tomato half over bowl, cut side down, and squeeze to remove seeds. Chop tomatoes. Set aside.

3. Melt margarine in large Dutch oven over medium-high heat. Add onion and garlic; cook and stir 1 to 2 minutes until onion is tender. Add carrots and celery; cook and stir 7 to 9 minutes until tender.

4. Stir in tomatoes, broth, rice, tomato paste, Worcestershire sauce, dried thyme, black pepper and hot pepper sauce. Bring to a boil. Reduce heat to low. Cook about 30 minutes, stirring frequently.

5. Remove from heat. Let stand at room temperature to cool 10 minutes. Process soup in small batches in food processor or blender until smooth.

6. Return soup to Dutch oven. Bring to a boil over medium-high heat. Reduce heat to low. Simmer 3 to 5 minutes until heated through. Garnish, if desired.   *Makes 8 servings*

Step 2. Squeezing tomato half to remove seeds.

Step 5. Processing soup in food processor until smooth.

Cream of Avocado Soup

6 medium avocados
Lemon juice
1 cup dry white wine
4 eggs*
4 cups milk, divided
1 cup chicken broth
½ teaspoon salt
¼ teaspoon white pepper
3 cups sour cream, divided
Black caviar and ground red pepper for garnish

*Use clean, uncracked eggs.

1. To prepare avocados, place avocados on cutting board. Insert utility knife into stem end of each avocado; slice in half lengthwise to the pit, turning avocado while slicing. Remove knife blade; twist both halves to pull apart. Press knife blade into pit; twist knife to pull pit from avocado.

2. Scoop out meat leaving ¼-inch shell; set aside avocado meat. Lightly sprinkle shells with lemon juice to prevent browning. Cover; refrigerate.

3. Process avocado meat and wine in small batches in food processor or blender until smooth. Transfer to large bowl; set aside.

4. In top of double boiler, beat eggs with 2 cups milk. Heat slowly over hot, not boiling, water; stir until mixture is thick enough to coat back of spoon.

5. Remove from heat; stir in broth. Let stand at room temperature until cool.

6. Stir cooled egg mixture, salt and white pepper into avocado mixture. Mix in 2 cups sour cream, stirring until smooth. Add remaining 2 cups milk.

7. Process soup in small batches in food processor or blender until smooth. Adjust seasonings. Cover; refrigerate until very cold.

8. To serve, pour cold soup into avocado shells.

9. Top each portion with about 1 tablespoon of the remaining 1 cup sour cream. Garnish, if desired. *Makes 12 servings*

Step 1. Removing avocado pit.

Step 2. Scooping out avocado meat.

Step 4. Heating egg mixture until it coats back of spoon.

Chilly Cucumber Soup

4 large cucumbers
2 tablespoons butter or
  margarine
2 tablespoons all-purpose flour
¼ cup finely chopped fresh
  parsley (page 42)
¼ cup finely chopped celery leaves
1 envelope Lipton® Recipe
  Secrets™ Golden Onion
  Recipe Soup Mix
2 cups water
2 cups light cream or half-and-
  half
  Cucumber slices, celery leaves
  and lemon peel for garnish

1. Remove cucumber peels with paring knife or vegetable peeler. To seed cucumbers, cut in half lengthwise and scrape out seeds with a small spoon. Finely chop enough cucumbers to measure 3½ cups. Set aside.

2. Melt butter in large saucepan over medium heat. Stir in flour and cook 3 minutes, stirring constantly.

3. Add chopped cucumbers, parsley and chopped celery leaves. Reduce heat to low. Cook and stir until cucumbers are tender when pierced with fork, about 8 minutes.

4. Combine soup mix and water in small bowl; add to cucumber mixture. Bring to a boil over medium-high heat. Reduce heat to low. Simmer, covered, 15 minutes. Remove from heat. Let stand at room temperature until cool.

5. Process soup in small batches in blender or food processor until smooth.

6. Stir cream into soup. Cover; refrigerate. Serve soup cold. Garnish, if desired.

Makes about 6 servings

Step 1. Seeding cucumbers.

Step 3. Testing tenderness of cucumbers.

Step 5. Processing soup in blender until smooth.

"Dearhearts" Seafood Bisque

1 pound mixed shellfish (raw
   shrimp, raw scallops or
   canned crabmeat)
2 tablespoons olive oil
1 onion, finely chopped (page 14)
1 (9-ounce) package frozen
   artichoke hearts, thawed
2 cups chicken broth
½ cup white wine
1 cup heavy or whipping cream
2 tablespoons chopped fresh
   parsley (page 42)
1 teaspoon salt
½ teaspoon ground nutmeg
¼ teaspoon white pepper
   Additional chopped fresh
   parsley for garnish

1. To remove shells from shrimp, use your fingers to peel shell off the side with the legs. Lift it up and over, then back around to the leg side. Discard shells. Using paring knife, cut off and discard tail sections.

2. To devein shrimp, use paring knife to make a small cut along the back of the shrimp; lift out the dark vein with knife tip. (You may find this easier to do under cold running water.) Cut each shrimp into 3 to 4 smaller pieces, if desired. Set shrimp aside.

3. Heat oil in large skillet over medium-high heat. Add onion; cook and stir 5 minutes or until softened. Add artichokes, broth and wine. Bring to a boil over medium-high heat. Reduce heat to low. Simmer, covered, 5 to 7 minutes.

4. Process soup in small batches in food processor or blender until smooth. Return soup to saucepan.

5. Stir in shellfish, heavy cream, 2 tablespoons chopped parsley, salt, nutmeg and pepper. Bring soup just to a simmer over medium heat. Reduce heat to low. Simmer very gently, uncovered, 5 to 10 minutes. *Do not boil.* (Shellfish will become tough if soup boils.) Garnish, if desired.   *Makes 6 servings*

Step 1. Removing shells from shrimp.

Step 2. Deveining shrimp.

Step 3. Simmering broth mixture.

Sherried Oyster and Brie Soup

1 cup cream sherry
1 quart select Maryland oysters
   with liquor
2 tablespoons butter
1 pound fresh mushrooms, thinly
   sliced
½ cup minced shallots
2 tablespoons fresh lemon juice
2 tablespoons all-purpose flour
3 cups beef broth
4 ounces Brie cheese
1 cup milk
1 cup heavy or whipping cream
   Salt and white pepper to taste
   Fresh chives for garnish

1. Bring sherry to a boil in small saucepan over medium-high heat. Reduce heat to low. Simmer until slightly thickened and reduced to ½ cup. Set aside.

2. Drain oysters and reserve liquor. Set aside.

3. Melt butter in large saucepan over medium-high heat. When foam subsides, stir in mushrooms, shallots and lemon juice; cook and stir 2 minutes. Sprinkle with flour; cook and stir 1 minute more.

4. Add broth and reduced sherry; bring to a boil over medium-high heat. Reduce heat to low. Simmer 20 minutes.

5. Cut Brie cheese into wedges and, using paring knife, remove and discard outer white rind.

6. Add cheese to soup; stir to melt. Stir in reserved oyster liquor, milk and cream; season with salt and pepper. Heat until very hot. *Do not boil.*

7. Remove from heat; add oysters. Cover and let stand until oysters are just plumped. Garnish, if desired.   *Makes 4 servings*

Step 1. Simmering sherry until reduced by half.

Step 3. Sprinkling mushroom mixture with flour.

Step 5. Removing outer white rind from Brie cheese.

Southwest Appetizer Cheesecake

Tortilla chips
2 tablespoons margarine, melted
1 cup cottage cheese
**3 packages (8 ounces each)
 cream cheese, softened**
4 eggs
**2½ cups (10 ounces) shredded
 sharp natural Cheddar cheese**
**1 can (4 ounces) chopped green
 chilies, well drained**
**1 container (8 ounces) sour
 cream**
**1 container (8 ounces) jalapeño-
 Cheddar gourmet dip**
1 cup chopped tomatoes
½ cup chopped green onions
¼ cup sliced pitted ripe olives

1. Place tortilla chips in a large plastic food bag; seal. Finely crush chips with mallet or rolling pin to measure ⅔ cup.

2. Preheat oven to 325°F. Combine crushed chips and margarine; press onto bottom of 9-inch springform pan. Bake 15 minutes.

3. Meanwhile, process cottage cheese in food processor or blender until smooth. Beat cream cheese and cottage cheese in large bowl with an electric mixer at medium speed until well blended. Add eggs, 1 at a time, mixing well after each addition. Stir in Cheddar cheese and chilies. Pour mixture over baked crust. Return to oven; bake 60 minutes.

4. Combine sour cream and dip in small bowl; mix thoroughly. Remove cheesecake from oven and carefully pour sour cream mixture evenly over top. Return cheesecake to oven; bake 10 minutes more.

5. Remove cheesecake from oven. Let stand at room temperature to cool slightly. Loosen cake from rim of pan; cool completely before removing rim. Refrigerate cheesecake until ready to serve. Just before serving, top with tomatoes, green onions and olives. Cut into wedges to serve.

Makes 10 to 12 first-course servings

Step 1. Crushing tortilla chips.

Step 2. Pressing crust onto bottom of pan.

Step 4. Pouring sour cream mixture over top of baked chessecake.

Cheddar Chili Tomato Pots

6 medium tomatoes
3½ cups (14 ounces) Sargento®
   Fancy Supreme™ Shredded
   Sharp Cheddar Cheese,
   divided
2 cans (4 ounces each) chopped
   green chilies, well drained
½ teaspoon dried oregano leaves,
   crushed
½ teaspoon minced garlic
   (page 8)
6 tablespoons sour cream
3 green onions, sliced
   Breadsticks for serving

1. Preheat oven to 325°F. Grease 11×7-inch baking dish. Cut ½-inch slice from top of each tomato; scoop out pulp and seeds, leaving ¼-inch shell (save pulp for another use, such as salads or sauces).

2. Invert tomatoes on paper towel-lined plate; let drain 20 minutes.

3. Combine 3 cups cheese, chilies, oregano and garlic in medium bowl.

4. Using large spoon, stuff tomato shells with cheese mixture.

5. Arrange tomato shells in prepared dish. Bake 20 minutes. Top with sour cream, remaining ½ cup cheese and green onions. Serve with breadsticks.

Makes 6 first-course servings

Step 1. Scooping pulp and seeds out of tomatoes.

Step 2. Draining tomato shells.

Step 4. Stuffing tomato shells.

Plentiful "P's" Salad

4 cups fresh black-eyed peas
1½ cups uncooked rotini pasta
1 medium red bell pepper
1 medium green bell pepper
1 medium purple onion, chopped
   (page 42)
4 slices Provolone cheese,
   chopped
4 slices salami or pepperoni,
   chopped
1 jar (4½ ounces) whole
   mushrooms, drained
1 jar (2 ounces) chopped
   pimiento, drained
2 tablespoons chopped fresh
   parsley (page 42)
2 tablespoons dry Italian salad
   dressing mix
½ teaspoon salt
¼ teaspoon black pepper
½ cup wine vinegar
¼ cup sugar
¼ cup vegetable oil
   Onion slices and fresh herb
   sprigs for garnish

1. To cook black-eyed peas, place peas in large saucepan. Cover with water; bring to a boil over high heat. Reduce heat to low. Simmer, covered, until peas are soft when pierced with fork, 15 to 20 minutes. Drain and set aside.

2. Cook rotini according to package directions until tender but still firm. Drain and set aside.

3. Cut bell peppers in half through the stem. Trim and discard stems and white ribs. Remove seeds by scraping with knife, or by holding each bell pepper half under running water. Chop peppers into ¼ × ¼-inch pieces.

4. Combine black-eyed peas, pasta, bell peppers, chopped onion, Provolone cheese, salami, mushrooms, pimiento and parsley in large bowl; set aside.

5. Combine salad dressing mix, salt and black pepper in small bowl. Add vinegar and sugar; mix well. Whisk in oil.

6. Add oil mixture to black-eyed pea mixture. Toss lightly until well combined.

7. Cover; refrigerate at least 2 hours before serving. Garnish, if desired.

Makes 12 first-course servings

Note: Other vegetables such as cauliflower, broccoli, carrots or celery can be added.

Step 1. Testing tenderness of black-eyed peas.

Step 3. Scraping bell pepper with knife to remove seeds.

Step 5. Whisking oil into salad dressing mixture.

Jumbo Shells Seafood Fancies

1 package (16 ounces) uncooked
  jumbo pasta shells
1 can (7½ ounces) crabmeat
4 ounces (1 cup) grated Swiss
  cheese
1 can (2½ ounces) tiny shrimp,
  drained
½ cup salad dressing or
  mayonnaise
2 tablespoons thinly sliced celery
1 tablespoon finely chopped
  onion (page 42)
1 tablespoon finely chopped
  pimiento
  Celery leaves for garnish

1. Cook shells according to package directions until tender but still firm; drain. Rinse under cold running water; drain again.

2. Invert shells on paper towel-lined plate to drain and cool.

3. Drain and discard liquid from crabmeat. Place crabmeat in large bowl; flake with fork into small pieces. Remove any bits of shell or cartilage.

4. Add Swiss cheese, shrimp, salad dressing, celery, onion and pimiento to crabmeat. If mixture seems too dry, add more salad dressing.

5. Using large spoon, stuff cooled shells with seafood mixture. Cover; refrigerate until chilled. Garnish, if desired.

Makes 8 first-course servings

Step 1. Rinsing shells.

Step 2. Draining and cooling shells.

Step 5. Stuffing shells.

Fresh Tomato Pasta Andrew

2 cloves garlic
1 pound fresh tomatoes, cut into wedges
1 cup packed fresh basil leaves
2 tablespoons olive oil
8 ounces Camenzola cheese *or* 6 ounces ripe Brie cheese, cut into small pieces
2 ounces Stilton cheese, cut into small pieces
Salt and white pepper to taste
4 ounces uncooked angel hair pasta, vermicelli or other thin pasta
Freshly grated Parmesan cheese
Additional fresh basil leaves for garnish

1. Trim off ends of garlic cloves. To loosen garlic peels, crush cloves with flat side of a large knife. Remove peels and discard.* Chop garlic.

2. Place tomato wedges, 1 cup basil, garlic and oil in food processor or blender container; process until ingredients are roughly chopped, but not puréed.

3. Combine tomato mixture with Camenzola cheese and Stilton cheese in large bowl; season with salt and pepper.

4. Cook pasta according to package directions until tender but still firm; rinse and drain.

5. Top hot pasta with tomato-cheese mixture and serve with Parmesan cheese. Garnish, if desired.   *Makes 4 first-course servings*

*To peel garlic cloves in microwave, place cloves in small custard cup. Microwave at HIGH (100% power) until slightly softened, 10 to 20 seconds. Slip the cloves out of their skins.

Step 1. Crushing garlic clove to remove peel.

Step 2. Processing tomato mixture in food processor.

Step 4. Rinsing and draining pasta.

Chilled Seafood Lasagna with Herbed Cheese

8 (2-inch wide) uncooked lasagna noodles
2 cups Wisconsin ricotta cheese
1½ cups Wisconsin mascarpone cheese
2 tablespoons lemon juice
1 tablespoon minced fresh basil leaves
1 tablespoon minced dill
1 tablespoon minced fresh tarragon leaves
¼ teaspoon white pepper
1 pound lox, divided
4 ounces Whitefish caviar, gently rinsed
Lox and fresh tarragon sprigs for garnish

1. Cook lasagna noodles according to package directions until tender but still firm. Drain and set aside.

2. Process the ricotta cheese, mascarpone cheese, lemon juice, basil, dill, tarragon and pepper in food processor or blender until well combined.

3. Line terrine mold* with plastic wrap, allowing wrap to extend 5 inches over sides of pan.

4. Place 1 noodle in bottom of pan. Spread ½ cup cheese mixture over noodle. Cover cheese mixture with 2 ounces lox; spread 2 rounded teaspoons caviar over lox. Repeat layers with remaining ingredients, ending with noodle. Set aside remaining 2 ounces lox for garnish.

5. Cover; refrigerate several hours or until firm. Carefully lift lasagna from mold and remove plastic wrap.

6. Garnish with remaining strips of lox rolled to look like roses and fresh tarragon sprigs, if desired. Slice with warm knife.

Makes 24 first-course or 8 entrée servings

*Can be prepared without terrine mold. Layer lasagna on plastic wrap. Cover and wrap with foil.

Step 3. Lining terrine mold.

Step 4. Covering layer of cheese mixture with lox.

Step 6. Rolling strips of lox to look like roses.

Scampi alla "Fireman Chef"

1½ pounds large raw prawns
  (about 16)
6 tablespoons butter
4 tablespoons minced garlic
  (page 34)
6 green onions, thinly sliced
¼ cup dry white wine
  Juice of 1 lemon (about
  2 tablespoons)
8 large fresh parsley sprigs,
  finely chopped (page 42)
  Salt and black pepper to taste
  Lemon slices and fresh parsley
  sprigs for garnish

1. To remove shells from prawns, use your fingers to peel shell off the side with the legs. Lift it up and over, then back around to the leg side. Discard shells.

2. To devein prawns, use paring knife to make a small cut along the back of the prawns; lift out the dark vein with knife tip. (You may find this easier to do under cold running water.) Set prawns aside.

3. To clarify butter, melt butter in small saucepan over low heat. *Do not stir.* Skim off the white foam that forms on top. Strain clarified butter through a cheesecloth into glass measuring cup to yield ⅓ cup. Discard milky residue at bottom of pan.

4. Heat clarified butter in large skillet over medium heat. Add garlic; cook and stir 1 to 2 minutes until softened but not brown.

5. Add prawns, green onions, wine and lemon juice; cook and stir until prawns turn pink and are firm and opaque, 1 to 2 minutes on each side. *Do not overcook.*

6. Just before serving, add chopped parsley and season with salt and pepper. Serve on individual shell-shaped or small gratin dishes. Garnish, if desired.

Makes 8 first-course servings

Step 1. Removing shells from prawns.

Step 2. Deveining prawns.

Step 3. Straining clarified butter.

Egg Champignons

6 eggs
¼ cup dry bread crumbs
¼ cup (1 ounce) crumbled blue
  cheese
2 tablespoons thinly sliced green
  onions with tops
2 tablespoons dry white wine
2 tablespoons butter, melted
1 tablespoon chopped fresh
  parsley (page 42) *or* ½
  tablespoon dried parsley
  flakes
½ teaspoon garlic salt
24 large fresh mushroom caps
  (about 1½ inches in diameter)
  Paprika (optional)
  Green onions and tomato slices
  for garnish

1. To hard cook eggs, place the 6 eggs in a single layer in a saucepan. Add enough water to cover eggs by at least 1 inch. Cover and quickly bring water just to a boil over high heat. Turn off heat. If necessary, remove the pan from burner to prevent further boiling. Let eggs stand, covered, in hot water 15 to 17 minutes. Immediately run cold water over eggs or place in ice water until completely cooled.

2. Peel eggs by tapping all around the shell with a table knife to form a network of cracks. Peel shell away under cold running water. Finely chop eggs.

3. Preheat oven to 450°F. Lightly grease baking sheet. Combine eggs, bread crumbs, blue cheese, 2 tablespoons green onions, wine, butter, parsley and garlic salt in medium bowl.

4. Fill each mushroom cap with 1 rounded tablespoon egg mixture. Place mushroom caps on prepared baking sheet.

5. Bake 8 to 10 minutes. Sprinkle with paprika. Garnish, if desired.

Makes 8 first-course servings

Step 1. Hard-cooking eggs.

Step 2. Peeling eggs.

Step 4. Filling mushroom caps.

Spinach-Cheese Triangles

1 small onion
½ cup minced fresh parsley
3 packages (10 ounces each) frozen chopped spinach, thawed
¼ cup olive oil
2 eggs
16 ounces (1 pound) feta cheese, drained and crumbled
1 teaspoon dried oregano leaves, crushed *or* 2 tablespoons chopped fresh oregano leaves
   Freshly grated nutmeg to taste
   Salt and black pepper to taste
1 package (16 ounces) frozen phyllo dough, thawed to room temperature
2 cups margarine, melted

1. To chop onion in food processor, peel and quarter onion; place in bowl. Pulse 4 to 7 times until onion is finely chopped. Scrape bowl once during chopping. Chop enough onion to measure ½ cup. Drain onions, if needed. Set aside. (See page 14 for chopping technique with knife.)

2. To mince parsley, place parsley in 1-cup measuring cup. Snip enough parsley with kitchen scissors to measure ½ cup. Set aside.

3. To drain spinach, place spinach, 1 package at a time, in bottom of pie plate. Place another pie plate on top; over sink squeeze plates together and tilt slightly to press excess liquid from spinach. Set spinach aside.

4. Preheat oven to 375°F.

5. Heat oil over medium-high heat in small skillet. Add onion; cook and stir until translucent and golden.

continued on page 44

Step 1. Chopping onion in food processor.

Step 2. Snipping parsley to mince.

Step 3. Draining spinach.

Spinach-Cheese Triangles, continued

6. Beat eggs in large bowl with an electric mixer at medium-high speed until light and lemon colored.

7. Stir in onion with oil, feta cheese, parsley, oregano and spinach. Season with nutmeg, salt and pepper.

8. Remove phyllo from package; unroll and place on large sheet of waxed paper. Fold phyllo crosswise into thirds. Use scissors to cut along folds into thirds.

9. Cover phyllo with large sheet of plastic wrap and damp, clean kitchen towel. (Phyllo dries out quickly if not covered.)

10. Lay 1 strip of phyllo at a time on a flat surface and brush immediately with melted butter. Fold strip in half lengthwise. Brush with butter again. Place rounded teaspoonful of spinach filling on 1 end of strip; fold over 1 corner to make triangle.

11. Continue folding end to end, as you would fold a flag, keeping edges straight.

12. Brush top with butter. Repeat process until all filling is used up.

13. Place triangles in a single layer, seam-side down, on ungreased jelly-roll pan. Bake 20 minutes or until lightly browned. Serve warm.

Makes 5 dozen appetizers

Step 8. Cutting phyllo into thirds.

Step 10. Folding one corner of phyllo over filling.

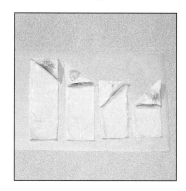

Step 11. Continuing to fold the length of the phyllo strip.

Cheesy Onion Focaccia

1 large red onion
½ cup *plus* 3 tablespoons honey, divided
2⅓ cups warm water (105° to 115°F), divided
1½ packages active dry yeast
6 tablespoons olive oil, divided
⅓ cup cornmeal
3 cups whole wheat flour
1½ tablespoons coarse salt
3 to 4 cups all-purpose flour, divided
1 cup red wine vinegar
Additional cornmeal
1 cup grated Parmesan cheese
½ teaspoon onion salt
Black pepper to taste

1. To slice onion, peel skin and cut onion in half through the root. Place, cut side down, on cutting board. Cut thin, vertical slices the length of the onion. Set aside.

2. To proof yeast, place 3 tablespoons honey in large bowl. Pour ⅓ cup water over honey. *Do not stir.* Sprinkle yeast over water. Let stand at room temperature about 15 minutes or until bubbly.*

3. Add remaining 2 cups water, 3 tablespoons olive oil, ⅓ cup cornmeal and whole wheat flour to yeast mixture; mix until well blended.

4. Stir in salt and 2 cups all-purpose flour. Gradually stir in enough remaining all-purpose flour until mixture clings to sides of bowl.

*If yeast does not bubble, it is no longer active. Discard yeast mixture and start again. Always check the expiration date on yeast packet. Also, water that is too hot will kill yeast; it is best to use a thermometer.

continued on page 46

Step 1. Slicing onion.

Step 2. Proofing yeast.

Step 4. Dough mixture clinging to sides of bowl.

Cheesy Onion Focaccia, continued

5. Turn dough out onto lightly floured surface. To knead in remaining flour, fold the dough in half toward you and press dough away from you with heels of hands. Give dough a quarter turn and continue folding, pushing and turning until the dough is smooth and satiny, about 10 minutes.

6. Divide dough into halves. Place each half in a large, lightly greased bowl; turn each dough half over to grease surface. Cover each with clean kitchen towel and let dough rise in warm place (85°F) until doubled in bulk. (Press two fingertips about ½ inch into dough. Dough is ready if indentations remain when fingers are removed.)

7. Meanwhile, combine onion, vinegar and remaining ½ cup honey. Marinate at room temperature at least 1 hour.

8. Grease 2 (12-inch) pizza pans and sprinkle with additional cornmeal. Stretch dough and pat into pans; create valleys with fingertips.

9. Cover dough with greased plastic wrap; let rise for 1 hour. Dough will double in size.

10. Preheat oven to 400°F.

11. Drain onions and scatter them over dough. Sprinkle with remaining 3 tablespoons olive oil, Parmesan cheese and onion salt; season with pepper.

12. Bake 25 to 30 minutes until flatbread is crusty and golden. Cut into wedges to serve. Serve warm.

Makes 2 breads (6 to 8 servings each)

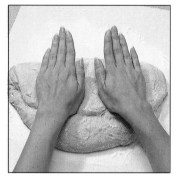

Step 5. Kneading dough.

Step 6. Testing dough that has doubled in bulk.

Step 8. Stretching and patting dough into pan.

Chinese Vegetable Rolls

¼ cup red wine
2 tablespoons teriyaki sauce
2 tablespoons Worcestershire sauce
1 cup diced zucchini
1 cup diced yellow squash
1 cup broccoli flowerets
1 cup cauliflower flowerets
½ cup diced carrots
¼ cup chopped red onion (page 42)
¼ cup chopped fresh parsley (page 42)
¼ teaspoon white pepper
¼ teaspoon garlic salt
⅛ teaspoon ground red pepper
⅛ teaspoon black pepper
1 package (16 ounces) egg roll wrappers
1 egg, beaten
Peanut or corn oil for frying
Sweet and sour sauce, hot mustard sauce or soy sauce for dipping

1. Combine wine, teriyaki sauce and Worcestershire sauce in large saucepan over medium heat. Stir in zucchini, squash, broccoli, cauliflower, carrots, red onion, parsley, white pepper, garlic salt, ground red pepper and black pepper. Cook and stir 5 to 6 minutes until flavors blend and vegetables are crisp-tender. *Do not overcook.*

2. Remove from heat. Immediately transfer vegetable mixture to bowl to prevent further cooking. Let stand at room temperature until cool.

3. Place about 2 tablespoons vegetable mixture on bottom half of 1 egg roll wrapper.

4. Moisten left and right edges of wrapper with egg. Fold bottom edge up to just cover filling.

5. Fold left and right edges over ½ inch; roll up jelly-roll fashion.

6. Moisten top edge with egg to seal. Repeat with remaining egg roll wrappers and vegetable filling.

7. Heat ½ inch oil in large, heavy saucepan over medium-high heat until oil reaches 365°F; adjust heat to maintain temperature. Fry egg rolls, a few at a time, in hot oil 2 minutes or until golden brown, turning once. Remove with slotted spoon; drain on paper towels.

8. Serve warm with sauces for dipping.

Makes about 15 appetizers

Step 4. Folding up bottom edge of egg roll wrapper.

Step 5. Rolling up egg roll wrapper, jelly-roll fashion.

Serbian Lamb Sausage Kabobs

1 pound lean ground lamb
1 pound lean ground beef
1 small onion, finely chopped (page 42)
2 cloves garlic, minced (page 52)
1 tablespoon hot Hungarian paprika
1 small egg, slightly beaten
Salt and black pepper to taste
3 to 4 red, green or yellow bell peppers, cut into squares
Rice pilaf for serving
Tomato slices and green onion brushes for garnish

1. Combine lamb, beef, finely chopped onion, garlic, paprika and egg in large bowl; season with salt and black pepper.

2. Place meat mixture on cutting board; pat evenly into 8 × 6-inch rectangle. With sharp knife, cut meat into 48 (1-inch) squares; shape each square into small oblong sausage.

3. Place sausages on waxed paper-lined jelly-roll pan and freeze 30 to 45 minutes or until firm. *Do not freeze completely.*

4. Alternately thread 3 sausages and 3 bell pepper pieces onto each metal skewer.

5. Grill over medium-hot coals 5 to 7 minutes. Turn kabobs, taking care not to knock sausages off. Continue grilling 5 to 7 minutes longer until meat is done. Serve with rice pilaf.

6. For green onion brushes, trim root and most of green top from green onions. Using sharp scissors, make parallel cuts, about 1½ inches long, along length of each onion at the root end or both ends. Fan out the cuts to form a brush. If desired, place brushes in bowl of ice water for several hours to open and curl. Place green onion brush and several tomato slices on each plate, if desired.

Makes 8 servings or 16 kabobs

Note: The seasonings may be adjusted, but the key to authenticity is the equal parts of beef and lamb and the garlic and paprika. You may use sweet paprika if you prefer a milder taste.

Step 2. Shaping meat squares into oblong sausages.

Step 4. Alternately threading sausages and pepper pieces onto skewers.

Step 6. Cutting green onions into brushes.

Patrician Escargots

4 **heads garlic,* separated into cloves**
½ **cup olive oil**
½ **cup butter**
1 **onion, finely chopped (page 42)**
1 **teaspoon finely chopped fresh rosemary leaves** *or* ½ **teaspoon dried rosemary leaves, crushed**
¼ **teaspoon dried thyme leaves, crushed**
2 **dashes ground nutmeg**
Salt and black pepper to taste
24 **large canned snails, drained**
½ **cup chopped fresh parsley (page 42)**
24 **large fresh mushrooms**
12 **pieces thin-sliced white bread for serving**

*The whole garlic bulb is called a head.

1. Trim off ends of garlic cloves. To loosen garlic peels, crush cloves with flat side of a large knife. Remove peels and discard.** Finely chop garlic.

2. Heat oil and butter in large skillet over medium heat until butter is melted. Add garlic, onion, rosemary, thyme and nutmeg; season with salt and pepper. Reduce heat to low. Add snails and parsley to garlic mixture. Cook 30 minutes, stirring occasionally.

3. Preheat oven to 350°F. Remove stems from mushrooms and discard.

4. Arrange mushroom caps upside down in 2-inch-deep baking dish; place 1 snail from garlic mixture in each mushroom cap. Pour garlic mixture over snails; cover with foil and bake 30 minutes.

5. Meanwhile, remove crusts from bread slices. Toast each slice and cut diagonally into 4 triangles. Serve with escargots.

Makes 4 servings

**To peel garlic cloves in microwave, place the desired number of cloves in small custard cup. Microwave at HIGH (100% power) until slightly softened, 5 to 10 seconds for 1 clove or 45 to 55 seconds for a whole head. Slip the cloves out of their skins.

Step 1. Crushing garlic clove to remove peel.

Step 2. Adding drained snails to garlic mixture.

Step 4. Placing snails in mushroom caps.

Taco Dip

12 ounces cream cheese, softened
½ cup dairy sour cream
2 teaspoons chili powder
1½ teaspoons ground cumin
⅛ teaspoon ground red pepper
½ cup salsa
   Crisp salad greens
1 cup (4 ounces) shredded
   Wisconsin Cheddar cheese
1 cup (4 ounces) shredded
   Wisconsin Monterey Jack
   cheese
½ cup diced plum tomatoes
⅓ cup sliced green onions
¼ cup sliced pitted ripe olives
¼ cup sliced pimiento-stuffed
   green olives
   Tortilla chips and blue corn
   chips for serving

1. Combine cream cheese, sour cream, chili powder, cumin and ground red pepper in large bowl; mix until well blended. Stir in salsa.

2. Spread dip onto greens-lined 10-inch serving platter.

3. Top with Cheddar cheese, Monterey Jack cheese, tomatoes, green onions, ripe olives and green olives.

4. Serve with tortilla chips and blue corn chips.   *Makes 10 servings*

Step 1. Combining salsa and cream cheese mixture.

Step 2. Spreading dip onto greens lined platter.

Step 3. Sprinkling dip with toppings.

Microwave Oriental Relish Dip

1 cup peeled chopped tomatoes
(page 16)

¼ cup soy sauce

¼ cup drained canned crushed
pineapple

1 tablespoon firmly packed
brown sugar

1 tablespoon finely chopped red
bell pepper

1 tablespoon finely chopped
green onion

1 tablespoon minced garlic
(page 52)

2 teaspoons fresh lime juice

1½ teaspoons grated fresh ginger
(page 84)

2 teaspoons rice wine vinegar

1 teaspoon sesame oil

1 teaspoon arrowroot *or* 1½
teaspoons cornstarch

2 teaspoons cold water

2 (8-ounce) packages cream
cheese, softened

1 cup canned cream of coconut

1 cup creamy peanut butter

2 tablespoons fresh lime juice

¼ teaspoon ground red pepper

¼ teaspoon ground cardamom

8 cups assorted fresh vegetables
for serving

1. Combine tomatoes, soy sauce, pineapple, sugar, bell pepper, onion, garlic, 2 teaspoons lime juice and ginger in 1-quart glass measuring cup.

2. Microwave at HIGH (100% power) 8 minutes, stirring every 2 minutes. Stir in vinegar and oil. Microwave 5 to 6 minutes until tomato mixture is reduced to 1 cup.

3. Combine arrowroot and water in small dish; stir until well blended. Add to tomato mixture; stir well. Let stand at room temperature to cool slightly. Store relish, covered, in glass container in refrigerator.

4. To make dip, combine cream cheese and cream of coconut in large bowl; add relish and peanut butter . Mix until thoroughly combined. Add 2 tablespoons lime juice, ground red pepper and cardamom; stir until well blended. Serve with assorted vegetables.

Makes 16 servings

Note: Relish is also great mixed with reduced-calorie mayonnaise and used as a sandwich spread or salad dressing.

Step 1. Combined ingredients in 1-quart glass measuring cup.

Step 2. Reduced tomato mixture.

Southwestern Snack Squares

1¼ cups all-purpose flour
1 cup thinly sliced green onions
¾ cup Quaker® Enriched Corn Meal
1 tablespoon firmly packed brown sugar
2 teaspoons baking powder
1 teaspoon dried oregano leaves, crushed
½ teaspoon ground cumin
¼ teaspoon salt (optional)
1 cup milk
¼ cup vegetable oil
1 egg
1 cup (4 ounces) shredded Cheddar cheese
1 can (4 ounces) chopped green chilies, well drained
¼ cup finely chopped red bell pepper
2 slices crisp-cooked bacon, crumbled

1. Preheat oven to 400°F. Grease 11 × 7-inch baking dish. Combine flour, green onions, corn meal, brown sugar, baking powder, oregano, cumin and salt in large bowl; mix well.

2. Combine milk, oil and egg in small bowl. Add to corn meal mixture; mix just until moistened.

3. Spread evenly into prepared dish.

4. Combine cheese, chilies, bell pepper and bacon in medium bowl. Sprinkle evenly over corn meal mixture.

5. Bake 25 to 30 minutes until wooden toothpick inserted into center comes out clean. Let stand at room temperature to cool 10 minutes before cutting.

Makes about 15 pieces

Note: Also great served as a side dish to fish, chicken or pork—just cut into 8 pieces.

Step 1. Combining dry ingredients.

Step 2. Combining dry ingredients with liquid ingredients.

Step 4. Sprinkling cheese mixture over corn meal mixture.

Chicken 'n' Rice Pizza

4 cups cooked rice
½ cup ground walnuts (optional)
1½ cups (6 ounces) shredded Swiss cheese, divided
½ cup grated Parmesan cheese, divided
1 egg, beaten
2 tablespoons olive oil
2 boneless skinless chicken breast halves (about 6 ounces each), cut into bite-size pieces
1 small onion, sliced (page 45)
½ green bell pepper, sliced
½ red bell pepper, sliced
¼ pound fresh mushrooms, sliced
½ cup sliced pitted ripe olives
1 jar (14 ounces) pizza sauce
1 teaspoon dried basil leaves, crushed
1 teaspoon dried oregano leaves, crushed
1 cup (4 ounces) shredded mozzarella cheese

1. Preheat oven to 375°F. Combine rice, walnuts, ½ cup Swiss cheese, ¼ cup Parmesan cheese and egg in large bowl.

2. Press cheese mixture evenly onto bottom and ½ inch up side of greased 14-inch pizza pan. Bake 10 minutes. Let stand at room temperature until cool.

3. Heat oil in large skillet over medium-high heat. Add chicken, onion, bell peppers, mushrooms and olives. Cook and stir 7 minutes or until chicken is no longer pink in center; drain off excess liquid.

4. Spread pizza sauce over cooled rice crust. Spread remaining 1 cup Swiss cheese over sauce. Spread chicken mixture over cheese. Sprinkle with herbs.

5. Top pizza with mozzarella cheese and remaining ¼ cup Parmesan cheese. Bake 15 to 20 minutes. Remove from oven. Let stand at room temperature to cool slightly before serving.

Makes about 16 appetizer servings or 6 main-dish servings

Step 2. Pressing crust onto bottom and ½-inch up side of pan.

Step 3. Cooking and stirring chicken mixture.

Step 4. Spreading chicken mixture over cheese.

Oven-Fried California Quesadillas

½ cup chopped almonds
2½ cups (10 ounces) shredded Monterey Jack cheese
1 jar (6 ounces) marinated artichoke hearts, drained and chopped
1 can (2¼ ounces) sliced pitted ripe olives, drained
⅔ cup Pace® picante sauce
¼ cup loosely packed, chopped cilantro
8 flour tortillas (7 to 8 inch), divided
3 tablespoons butter or margarine, melted
Additional Pace® picante sauce for serving
Lime wedges for garnish

1. To toast almonds, preheat oven to 325°F. Place almonds in a single layer on baking sheet. Bake 8 to 10 minutes until golden, shaking pan or stirring occasionally to ensure even toasting. Let stand at room temperature until cool. (Almonds will darken and become crisper as they cool.)

2. *Increase oven temperature to 450°F.* Combine cheese, artichokes, olives, ⅔ cup picante sauce, almonds and cilantro in large bowl; mix well.

3. Brush one side of 4 tortillas with butter; place, buttered side down, on baking sheet.

4. Place 1 cup cheese mixture on top of each tortilla on baking sheet; spread to within ¾ inch of edge. Top each with 1 of the remaining tortillas, pressing firmly.

5. Brush tops of filled tortillas with butter.

6. Bake 10 minutes or until tops are lightly browned. Remove from oven. Let stand at room temperature to cool 3 to 5 minutes. Cut each quesadilla into 8 wedges.

7. Serve with additional picante sauce. Garnish, if desired.   *Makes 32 appetizers*

Step 1. Toasted almonds.

Step 3. Placing tortillas, buttered side down, on baking sheet.

Step 4. Pressing remaining tortillas over filling.

Southwestern Chilies Rellenos

2 cans (4 ounces each) whole green chilies, well drained
2 tablespoons olive oil
½ teaspoon white pepper
½ teaspoon salt
½ teaspoon ground red pepper
¼ teaspoon ground cloves
1½ cups (6 ounces) shredded Wisconsin Cheddar cheese
1½ cups (6 ounces) shredded Wisconsin Monterery Jack cheese
1 package (16 ounces) egg roll wrappers
1 egg yolk
1 teaspoon water
Vegetable oil

1. To seed chilies, cut each chili in half lengthwise using scissors or knife. Carefully scrape out and discard seeds. Rinse chilies well; drain. Pat dry with paper towels. (Wear rubber gloves when handling chilies to prevent irritation to your hands.)

2. Combine olive oil, white pepper, salt, ground red pepper and cloves in small bowl. Add chilies; toss to coat. Let stand at room temperature 1 hour. Combine Cheddar cheese and Monterey Jack cheese in another small bowl.

3. For each chili relleno, place 1 chili half in center of 1 egg roll wrapper; top with ¼ cup cheese mixture. Beat egg yolk and water in small cup; brush edges of egg roll wrapper with egg mixture.

4. Fold two opposite edges over filling, overlapping edges; press together, working out any air bubbles. Press ends together. Fold ends under and pinch to seal. Repeat with remaining chilies, egg roll wrappers and cheese mixture.

5. Heat ½ inch vegetable oil in large, heavy saucepan over medium-high heat until oil reaches 375°F; adjust heat to maintain temperature. Fry chilies rellenos, a few at a time, in hot oil 2 to 3 minutes until golden brown, turning once. Remove with slotted spoon; drain on paper towels.

Makes 6 servings

Step 1. Scraping seeds out of chilies.

Step 3. Brushing edges of egg roll wrapper with egg yolk mixture.

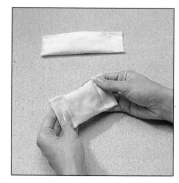
Step 4. Pinching ends of egg roll wrappers to seal.

Baked Garlic Bundles

**3 large heads garlic,* separated
   into cloves**
**¹/₂ of 16-ounce package frozen
   phyllo dough, thawed to room
   temperature**
³/₄ cup butter, melted
¹/₂ cup finely chopped walnuts
1 cup Italian-style bread crumbs

*The whole garlic bulb is called a head.

1. Trim off ends of garlic cloves. To loosen garlic peels, crush cloves with flat side of a large knife. Remove peels and discard.** Set garlic aside. (Technique on page 52.)

2. Preheat oven to 350°F. Remove phyllo from package; unroll and place on large sheet of waxed paper. Use scissors to cut phyllo crosswise into 2-inch-wide strips.

3. Cover phyllo with large sheet of plastic wrap and damp, clean kitchen towel. (Phyllo dries out quickly if not covered.)

4. Lay 1 strip of phyllo at a time on a flat surface and brush immediately with melted butter. Place 1 clove of garlic at one end. Sprinkle about 1 teaspoon walnuts along length of strip.

5. Roll up garlic clove and walnuts in strip, tucking in side edges as you roll.

6. Brush bundle with more butter. Roll in bread crumbs.

7. Repeat with remaining phyllo strips, garlic cloves, walnuts and butter until all but the smallest garlic cloves are used. Place bundles on rack in shallow roasting pan. Bake 20 minutes.   *Makes 24 to 27 appetizers*

**To peel garlic cloves in microwave, place the desired number of cloves in small custard cup. Microwave at HIGH (100% power) until slightly softened, 5 to 10 seconds for 1 clove or 45 to 55 seconds for a whole head. Slip the cloves out of their skins.

Step 2. Cutting phyllo crosswise into 2-inch-wide strips.

Step 4. Sprinkling walnuts along length of phyllo strip.

Step 5. Rolling up the length of the phyllo strip.

Cheesy Sun Crisps

2 cups (8 ounces) shredded
   Cheddar cheese
½ cup grated Parmesan cheese
½ cup sunflower oil margarine,
   softened
3 tablespoons water
1 cup all-purpose flour
¼ teaspoon salt (optional)
1 cup uncooked quick-cooking
   oats
⅔ cup roasted salted sunflower
   kernels

1. Beat Cheddar cheese, Parmesan cheese, margarine and water in large bowl with an electric mixer at medium speed until well blended. Add flour and salt; mix well.

2. Stir in oats and sunflower kernels; mix until well combined.

3. Shape dough into 12-inch-long roll; wrap securely in plastic wrap.

4. Refrigerate at least 4 hours. (Dough may be stored up to 1 week in refrigerator.)

5. Preheat oven to 400°F. Lightly grease cookie sheets. Cut roll into ⅛- to ¼-inch slices; flatten each slice slightly.

6. Place on prepared cookie sheets. Bake 8 to 10 minutes until edges are light golden brown. Remove immediately to wire racks. Let stand at room temperature until cool.

Makes 4 to 5 dozen crackers

Step 2. Stirring oats and sunflower kernels into cheese mixture.

Step 3. Shaping dough into 12-inch-long roll.

Step 5. Cutting roll into ⅛- to ¼-inch slices.

Harvest-Time Popcorn

2 tablespoons vegetable oil
1 cup popcorn kernels
2 cans (1¾ ounces each)
    shoestring potatoes (3 cups)
1 cup salted mixed nuts or
    peanuts
¼ cup margarine, melted
1 teaspoon dill weed
1 teaspoon Worcestershire sauce
½ teaspoon lemon-pepper
    seasoning
¼ teaspoon garlic powder
¼ teaspoon onion salt

1. Heat oil in 4-quart saucepan over high heat until hot. Add popcorn kernels. Cover pan; shake continously over heat until popping stops. Popcorn should measure 2 quarts. *Do not add butter or salt.*

2. Preheat oven to 325°F. Combine popcorn, shoestring potatoes and nuts in large roasting pan. Set aside.

3. Combine margarine, dill, Worcestershire sauce, lemon-pepper seasoning, garlic powder and onion salt in small bowl.

4. Pour evenly over popcorn mixture, stirring until evenly coated.

5. Bake 8 to 10 minutes, stirring once. Let stand at room temperature until cool. Store in airtight containers. *Makes 2½ quarts*

Step 2. Adding nuts to popcorn mixture.

Step 4. Pouring margarine mixture evenly over popcorn mixture.

Scallops à la Schaller

Fresh parsley
1 pound bacon, cut in half crosswise
2 pounds small sea scallops
½ cup olive oil
½ cup dry vermouth
1 teaspoon garlic powder
1 teaspoon black pepper
½ teaspoon onion powder
Dash of dried oregano leaves
Crisp salad greens
Lemon peel strips for garnish

1. To chop parsley, place parsley in 1-cup measuring cup. Snip enough parsley with kitchen scissors to measure 2 tablespoons. Set aside. (Technique on page 42.)

2. Wrap 1 bacon piece around each scallop; secure with wooden toothpicks, if necessary. Place wrapped scallops in 13 × 9-inch baking dish.

3. Combine olive oil, vermouth, parsley, garlic powder, pepper, onion powder and oregano in small bowl. Pour over wrapped scallops.

4. Marinate, covered, in refrigerator at least 4 hours.

5. Remove wrapped scallops from marinade. Arrange on rack of broiler pan. Broil, 4 inches from heat, 7 to 10 minutes until bacon is brown. Turn over; brown other side 5 minutes or until scallops are opaque.

6. Remove wooden toothpicks. Arrange on greens-lined platter. Garnish, if desired.

Makes 8 servings

Step 2. Wrapping bacon around scallops.

Step 3. Pouring olive oil mixture over wrapped scallops.

Step 5. Arranging wrapped scallops on rack of broiler pan.

Chilled Seafood Antipasto

7 tablespoons olive oil, divided
12 ounces sea scallops
2 teaspoons fresh lemon juice
1 pound cod fillets, cut into cubes
1 tablespoon sugar
1 tablespoon minced dry onion
1 teaspoon salt
1/2 teaspoon garlic powder
1/2 teaspoon black pepper
1/2 teaspoon crushed red pepper
   flakes
1 cup fresh basil leaves, divided
1 can (6 ounces) small pitted ripe
   olives, drained
1 jar (5 3/4 ounces) pimiento-
   stuffed Spanish green olives,
   drained
1 can (4 1/2 ounces) whole
   mushrooms, drained
1 can (8 1/2 ounces) artichoke
   hearts, drained
12 ounces white Cheddar cheese,
   cut into 1-inch chunks
1 cup vegetable oil
2/3 cup vinegar
   Crisp salad greens
   Additional fresh basil leaves for
   garnish

1. Heat 4 tablespoons olive oil in large nonstick skillet over high heat. Add scallops; cook and stir 2 to 4 minutes until scallops are opaque. Remove from heat. Stir in lemon juice. Set aside.

2. Heat remaining 3 tablespoons olive oil in another large nonstick skillet over high heat. Add cod; cook and stir 1 to 2 minutes until cod is opaque. Remove from heat. Set aside.

3. Combine sugar, onion, salt, garlic powder, black pepper and red pepper flakes in small bowl. Place 1/2 cup basil leaves in bottom of 13 × 9-inch dish; sprinkle with half the sugar mixture.

4. Add seafood; layer ripe olives, green olives, mushrooms, artichokes and cheese over seafood.

5. Top with remaining sugar mixture and 1/2 cup basil leaves. Combine vegetable oil and vinegar; pour over basil and seafood mixture.

6. Cover; refrigerate overnight. To serve, discard top layer of basil leaves. Using slotted spoon, remove seafood mixture from pan, discarding bottom layer of basil leaves. Place seafood mixture on greens-lined platter. Garnish, if desired. *Makes 8 servings*

Step 1. Cooking and stirring scallops until opaque.

Step 2. Cooking and stirring cod until opaque.

Step 3. Sprinkling 1/2 cup basil leaves with half the sugar mixture.

Mushrooms Mary Louise

6 medium cherrystone clams
3 medium raw shrimp
28 medium fresh mushroom caps, divided
8 tablespoons butter, divided
2 ounces scallops, diced
2 ribs celery, diced
¼ cup finely chopped onion (page 88)
⅓ cup white wine
⅔ cup bread crumbs
Hollandaise Sauce (page 78)
Celery slices for garnish

1. Discard any clams that remain open when tapped with fingers. To clean clams, scrub with stiff brush under cold running water. Soak clams in a mixture of ⅓ cup salt to 1 gallon water for 20 minutes. Drain water; repeat two more times.

2. Place clams on tray and refrigerate 1 hour to help clams relax. To shuck clams, take pointed clam knife in one hand and thick towel or glove in the other. With towel, grip shell in palm of hand. Keeping clam level with knife, insert tip of knife between the shell next to hinge; twist to pry shell until you hear a snap. (Use knife as leverage; do not force.)

3. Twist to open shell, keeping clam level at all times to save juice. Cut the muscle from the shell and discard top shell. Tip shell over strainer in bowl to catch clams; discard bottom shell. Strain clam juice from bowl through triple thickness of dampened cheesecloth. Set aside.

4. Chop clams into ¼ × ¼-inch pieces. Set aside.

5. To remove shells from shrimp, use your fingers to peel shell off the side with the legs. Lift it up and over, then back around to the leg side. Discard shells. Using paring knife, cut off and discard tail sections.

continued on page 78

Step 2. Shucking clams.

Step 3. Straining clam juice.

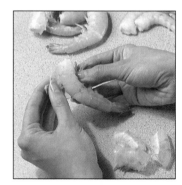

Step 5. Removing shells from shrimp.

Mushrooms Mary Louise, continued

6. To devein shrimp, use paring knife to make a small cut along the back of the shrimp; lift out the dark vein with knife tip. (You may find this easier to do under cold running water.) Chop shrimp into 1/4 × 1/4-inch pieces. Set aside.

7. Preheat oven to 350°F. Grease 4 (6-inch) casserole dishes. Slice 4 mushroom caps. Melt 1 tablespoon butter in large skillet over medium heat. Add sliced mushrooms; cook and stir until tender. Set aside.

8. Melt remaining 7 tablespoons butter in same skillet over medium heat. Add scallops, shrimp, diced celery and onion. Cook and stir over medium heat about 2 minutes or until shellfish is opaque. Add clams with reserved juice to skillet. Bring to a boil over medium-high heat. Reduce heat to low. Simmer 1 minute; add white wine. Remove from heat.

9. To fold in bread crumbs, sprinkle bread crumbs over shellfish mixture. Using rubber spatula, cut down through center of mixture, scrape across bottom of saucepan and up one side, using a fluid, lifting motion. Rotate the skillet a quarter turn and repeat until blended. (The mixture will become firm as it stands.)

10. Place 6 mushroom caps in each prepared casserole dish. Using small spoon, fill mushroom caps with stuffing

mixture. Bake 10 minutes.

11. Remove from oven. Place sliced mushrooms on top of each casserole. Top each with 1/4 cup of Hollandaise Sauce; return to oven just to heat through. Serve hot. Garnish, if desired.

Makes about 8 servings

Hollandaise Sauce

3 egg yolks
1 tablespoon cold water
1 cup unsalted butter, divided
1 to 1½ tablespoons fresh lemon juice
Dash ground red pepper

1. Place egg yolks and water in top of double boiler. Whisk until well combined.

2. Reserve 2 tablespoons butter. Heat remaining butter in small saucepan over low heat until just melted.

3. Add reserved 2 tablespoons butter to egg yolk mixture; place double boiler top over hot, not boiling, water. Whisk constantly until egg yolks thicken slightly.

4. Remove egg yolk mixture from heat. Gradually add melted butter to egg yolk mixture, whisking constantly.

5. Whisk in lemon juice and ground red pepper. Use sauce immediately.

Makes about 1 cup sauce

Step 6. Deveining shrimp.

Step 9. Folding bread crumbs into shellfish mixture.

Sesame-Sour Cream Meatballs

1 medium onion
¼ cup sesame seeds, divided
1 slice fresh bread
1½ pounds ground beef
¼ cup milk
1 egg
½ teaspoon salt
⅛ teaspoon black pepper
⅛ teaspoon ground ginger
4 tablespoons vegetable oil,
  divided
4 tablespoons butter or
  margarine, divided
1 cup beef broth, divided
Sesame-Sour Cream Sauce
  (page 80)
Fresh Italian parsley sprigs for
  garnish

1. To chop onion in food processor, peel and quarter onion; place in bowl. Pulse 4 to 7 times until onion is finely chopped. Scrape bowl once during chopping. Chop enough onion to measure ⅔ cup. Drain onions, if needed. Set aside. (See page 88 for chopping technique with knife.)

2. To toast sesame seeds, spread seeds in large, dry skillet. Shake skillet over medium-low heat until seeds begin to pop and turn golden, about 3 minutes. Set aside 2 tablespoons toasted sesame seeds for Sesame-Sour Cream Sauce.

3. Cut bread slice into quarters. Process bread quarters in food processor or blender until fine crumbs form. Crumbs should measure ½ cup.

4. Combine ground beef, onion, bread crumbs, milk, egg, salt, pepper and ginger in large bowl.

continued on page 80

Step 1. Chopping onion in food processor.

Step 2. Shaking skillet until sesame seeds begin to pop and turn golden.

Step 3. Processing bread until fine crumbs form.

Sesame-Sour Cream Meatballs, continued

5. Place meat mixture on cutting board; pat evenly into 8 × 6-inch rectangle. With sharp knife, cut meat into 48 (1-inch) squares; shape each square into 1-inch meatball.

6. Heat 2 tablespoons oil and 2 tablespoons butter in large skillet over medium heat. Cook half the meatballs until brown on all sides, 8 to 9 minutes. Add ½ cup broth. Bring to a boil over medium-high heat. Reduce heat to low. Simmer, covered, 5 to 10 minutes. Set cooked meatballs aside. Repeat with remaining meatballs, using remaining 2 tablespoons oil, 2 tablespoons butter and ½ cup broth.

7. Meanwhile, prepare Sesame-Sour Cream Sauce. Place hot meatballs in serving bowl; top with sauce. Sprinkle with remaining 2 tablespoons toasted sesame seeds. Garnish, if desired.

Makes 4 dozen meatballs

Sesame-Sour Cream Sauce

2 tablespoons butter or margarine
2 tablespoons all-purpose flour
½ teaspoon ground ginger
¼ teaspoon salt
½ cup beef broth
1 tablespoon soy sauce
2 tablespoons toasted sesame seeds
¾ cup sour cream

1. Melt butter in small saucepan over low heat. Blend in flour, ginger and salt. Cook and stir until bubbly, about 1 minute. Add beef broth. Cook until thickened, stirring constantly, for an additional minute. Add soy sauce and sesame seeds.

2. Remove from heat; pour into small bowl. Add sour cream, stirring until smooth. *Makes 1½ cups*

Step 5. Shaping meat squares into 1-inch meatballs.

Step 6. Cooking half the meatballs until brown on all sides.

Sesame-Sour Cream Sauce: Step 1. Cooking and stirring butter mixture until bubbly.

Turkey-Cheese Surprises

1 pound ground turkey
½ cup stuffing mix
½ cup finely chopped tart apple
½ cup plus 2 tablespoons grated
    Parmesan cheese, divided
½ teaspoon poultry seasoning
    Garlic salt to taste
    Black pepper to taste
1 tablespoon butter or margarine
½ cup finely chopped onion
    (page 88)
2 eggs
¼ cup Polly-O® ricotta cheese
4 ounces Polly-O® mozzarella
    cheese, cut into ½-inch cubes
1 cup dry bread crumbs
    Vegetable oil for frying
    Cranberry sauce for serving
    Orange twists,* orange peel
    and fresh sage sprigs for
    garnish

*To make orange twists, cut orange into thin slices. Cut slit through slices to centers. Twist slices from slits in opposite directions.

1. Combine turkey, stuffing mix, apple, 2 tablespoons Parmesan cheese and poultry seasoning in large bowl; season with garlic salt and pepper.

2. Heat butter in small skillet over medium-high heat. Add onion; cook and stir until onion is tender but not brown. Add onion with butter, eggs and ricotta cheese to turkey mixture; blend well. If mixture seems too dry, add a little milk.

3. For each meatball, shape small amount of turkey mixture around a cube of mozzarella cheese.

4. Mix bread crumbs and remaining ½ cup Parmesan cheese in large, shallow dish. Roll cheese-filled meatballs in mixture to coat well.

5. Heat ¼ inch oil in large, heavy saucepan over medium-high heat. Cook meatballs, a few at a time, until brown on all sides, 4 to 5 minutes. Remove with slotted spoon; drain on paper towels.

6. Serve with cranberry sauce. Garnish, if desired. *Makes about 2 dozen meatballs*

Step 2. Blending turkey mixture.

Step 3. Shaping turkey mixture around cube of mozarella cheese.

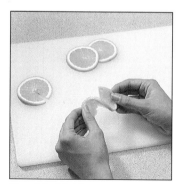

Garnish: Making orange twists.

Hot 'n' Honeyed Chicken Wings

1 **small piece fresh ginger**
1 **orange**
3 **pounds chicken wings**
¾ **cup Pace® picante sauce**
⅔ **cup honey**
⅓ **cup soy sauce**
¼ **cup Dijon-style mustard**
3 **tablespoons vegetable oil**
  Additional Pace® picante sauce
  Fresh Italian parsley sprigs for garnish

1. To grate fresh ginger, remove tough outer skin with sharp knife or vegetable peeler. Grate ginger using a ginger grater or the finest side of a box-shaped grater. Grate enough ginger to measure 2 tablespooons. Set aside.

2. To grate orange peel, rinse orange under running water. Grate orange peel using the finest side of a box-shaped grater, being careful to remove only the outermost layer of skin and not any of the bitter, white pith. Grate enough peel to measure ½ teaspoon. Set aside.

3. Cut off and discard wing tips from chicken. Cut each wing in half at joint.

4. Place chicken wings in 13×9-inch baking dish. Combine ¾ cup picante sauce, honey, soy sauce, mustard, oil, ginger and orange peel in small bowl; mix well. Pour over chicken wings.

5. Marinate, covered, in refrigerator at least 6 hours or overnight.

6. Preheat oven to 400°F. Drain marinade; reserve. Place chicken wings in single layer on foil-lined, 15×10-inch jelly-roll pan. Pour reserved marinade evenly over chicken wings. Bake 40 to 45 minutes until brown. Serve warm with additional picante sauce. Garnish, if desired. *Makes about 34 appetizers*

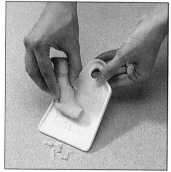

Step 1. Grating fresh ginger.

Step 2. Grating orange peel.

Step 3. Cutting chicken wings in half at joint.

Deep Fried Stuffed Shells

16 uncooked jumbo pasta shells
2 eggs, divided
1 can (6½ ounces) tuna, drained
   and flaked *or* 1 can (6 ounces)
   crabmeat, drained, flaked and
   cartilage removed
1 cup (4 ounces) shredded
   Cheddar or Swiss cheese
1 medium tomato, peeled, seeded
   and chopped (page 16)
2 tablespoons sliced green onions
½ teaspoon dried basil leaves,
   crushed
⅛ teaspoon black pepper
1 tablespoon water
1 cup dry bread crumbs
   Vegetable oil for frying
   Tartar sauce for serving
   Crisp salad greens, carrot curls
   and dill sprigs for garnish

1. Cook shells according to package directions until tender but still firm; drain. Rinse under cold running water; drain again.

2. Invert shells on paper towel-lined plate to cool. (Technique on page 32.)

3. Slightly beat 1 egg in large bowl. Add tuna, cheese, tomato, green onions, basil and pepper; mix well.

4. Using large spoon, stuff cooled shells with tuna mixture.

5. Beat remaining 1 egg with water in small bowl. Place bread crumbs in large, shallow dish. Dip each stuffed shell in egg mixture and roll in bread crumbs.

6. Heat 2 inches oil in large, heavy saucepan over medium-high heat until oil reaches 365°F; adjust heat to maintain temperature. Fry shells, a few at a time, in hot oil 1½ to 2 minutes until golden brown, turning once. Remove with slotted spoon; drain on paper towels.

7. Serve with tartar sauce. Garnish, if desired.

Makes 8 servings

Step 4. Stuffing pasta shells.

Step 5. Rolling shells in bread crumbs.

Step 6. Frying shells until golden brown.

Twelve Carat Black-Eyed Pea Relish

12 small carrots, peeled
1 sweet onion
1 cup vinegar
¼ cup vegetable oil
2 cans (15 ounces each) black-eyed peas, drained
1 green bell pepper, finely chopped
1 cup sugar
¼ cup Worcestershire sauce
2 teaspoons black pepper
2 teaspoons salt (optional)
2 dashes ground red pepper
Fresh basil leaves for garnish

1. To steam carrots, place half the carrots in folding metal steamer or colander. Place steamer over a few inches of water in a 2- or 3-quart saucepan with tight-fitting lid. (Be sure the steamer is at least 1 inch above the water.) Cover; bring the water to a boil. Steam carrots until crisp-tender, 16 to 18 minutes, adding more water to saucepan if necessary to prevent saucepan from boiling dry. Carefully remove carrots from steamer; repeat with remaining carrots. Coarsely chop cooled carrots. Set aside.

2. Peel skin from onion; cut in half through the root. Place, cut side down, on cutting board. To finely chop onion, hold knife horizontally. Make cuts parallel to board, almost to root end. Make vertical, lengthwise cuts of desired thickness. Slice across cuts to root end. (The closer the cuts are spaced, the finer the onion is chopped.) Set aside. (See page 92 for chopping technique with food processor.)

3. Combine vinegar and oil in small saucepan. Bring to a boil.

4. Combine black-eyed peas, carrots, onion, bell pepper, sugar, Worcestershire sauce, black pepper, salt and ground red pepper in large bowl.

5. Pour oil mixture over vegetable mixture.

6. Marinate, covered, in refrigerator at least 24 hours. Store, covered, in clean glass jars in refrigerator. Serve cold. Garnish, if desired.

Makes 2 to 3 pints

Step 1. Steaming carrots.

Step 2. Chopping onion with knife.

Step 5. Pouring oil mixture over vegetable mixture.

Shrimp Mold

1 can (7½ ounces) crabmeat
3 envelopes unflavored gelatin
¾ cup water
1 can (10¾ ounces) cream of shrimp soup
1 package (8 ounces) cream cheese, cut into cubes
2 cans (2½ ounces each) shrimp, drained
3 cups cooked Riceland® Rice
1 medium onion, chopped (page 88)
1 red bell pepper, chopped
1 cup mayonnaise
¼ cup lemon juice
2 tablespoons Worcestershire sauce
1 tablespoon garlic powder
1 teaspoon black pepper
    Crisp salad greens
    Crackers for serving
    Lemon and lime slices and fresh mint sprig for garnish

1. Drain and discard liquid from crabmeat. Place crabmeat in small bowl; flake with fork into small pieces. Remove any bits of shell or cartilage. Set aside.

2. To soften gelatin, sprinkle gelatin over water in small bowl. Let stand 1 minute.

3. Heat soup over medium heat in large saucepan; add gelatin mixture and stir to dissolve.

4. Add cream cheese and stir until melted. Remove from heat.

5. Add crabmeat, shrimp, rice, onion, red bell pepper, mayonnaise, lemon juice, Worcestershire sauce, garlic powder and black pepper; mix well.

6. Lightly spray 6-cup mold with nonstick vegetable cooking spray. Pour gelatin mixture into prepared mold and refrigerate until firm.

7. To unmold, pull gelatin mixture from edge of mold with moist fingers, or run small metal spatula or pointed knife dipped in warm water around edge of gelatin mixture. (Mold can also be dipped just to the rim in warm water for 10 seconds.) Carefully invert mold onto greens-lined plate. Shake mold and plate to loosen gelatin. Gently remove mold. Serve with favorite crackers. Garnish, if desired.

Makes 1 mold

Step 2. Softening gelatin.

Step 6. Pouring gelatin mixture into prepared mold.

Step 7. Pulling gelatin mixture away from edge of mold.

Liptauer Cheese Appetizer

1 medium onion
1 cup Polly-O® ricotta cheese
2 packages (3 ounces each) cream cheese, softened
2 tablespoons grated Parmesan cheese
2 tablespoons dry vermouth or gin
1 tablespoon drained capers
1½ teaspoons caraway seeds
2 anchovy fillets, mashed *or* 2 teaspoons anchovy paste
1 teaspoon dry mustard
1 teaspoon paprika
Red cabbage or bell pepper for serving container
Fresh herb sprigs for garnish

1. To chop onion in food processor, peel and quarter onion; place in bowl. Pulse 4 to 7 times until onion is finely chopped. Scrape bowl once during chopping. Drain onions, if needed. Set aside. (See page 88 for chopping technique with knife.)

2. Beat ricotta cheese and cream cheese in large bowl with an electric mixer on medium speed until well blended.

3. Stir in onion, Parmesan cheese, vermouth, capers, caraway seeds, anchovies, dry mustard and paprika; mix well.

4. Cover; refrigerate at least 1 day or up to 1 week to allow flavors to blend.

5. Just before serving, prepare cabbage or bell pepper for serving container. Discard any damaged outer leaves from cabbage. With sharp knife, slice small portion from bottom so cabbage will sit flat. Using knife, carefully cut out and remove inside portion of cabbage, leaving a 1-inch-thick shell. (Be careful not to cut through bottom of cabbage.) For bell pepper, cut ¼ to ½ inch off top and discard. Trim small portion off bottom so pepper will sit flat. Scoop out seeds and white ribs with spoon.

6. Spoon dip into hollowed-out cabbage or bell pepper. Or, spoon dip into small glass bowl and place in cabbage. Garnish, if desired.

Makes about 2 cups

Step 1. Chopping onion in food processor.

Step 5. Cutting out and removing inside portion of red cabbage.

Step 6. Spooning dip into hollowed-out red cabbage.

INDEX